The Honest Truth

Using the ACR
to explore
Alcohol Dependency

Nick Charles

HAWKSMOOR
PUBLISHING

First published 2021 by Hawksmoor Publishing

Kemp House, 152-160 City Rd, London, EC1V 2NX

www.hawksmoorpublishing.com

ISBN: 978-1-914066-04-7

Who is Nick Charles?

Nick Charles MBE was the first person in the UK to be honoured by the Queen *'for services to people with alcohol problems'*. His work, over 50 years, has become the most decorated in the UK alcohol treatment field.

He welcomes you to the ACR and describes it in his own words.

About the Examples

A number of actual case studies concerning the use of the ACR have been included in this book. To maintain anonymity, names and personal details have been changed.

Table of Contents

This Book

The aim of this book is to shine a light on your alcohol consumption so that *you* can decide whether you need to change your drinking patterns.

We do this by employing a six-week programme made up of periods when you are free to drink alcohol, and periods when you must try to abstain.

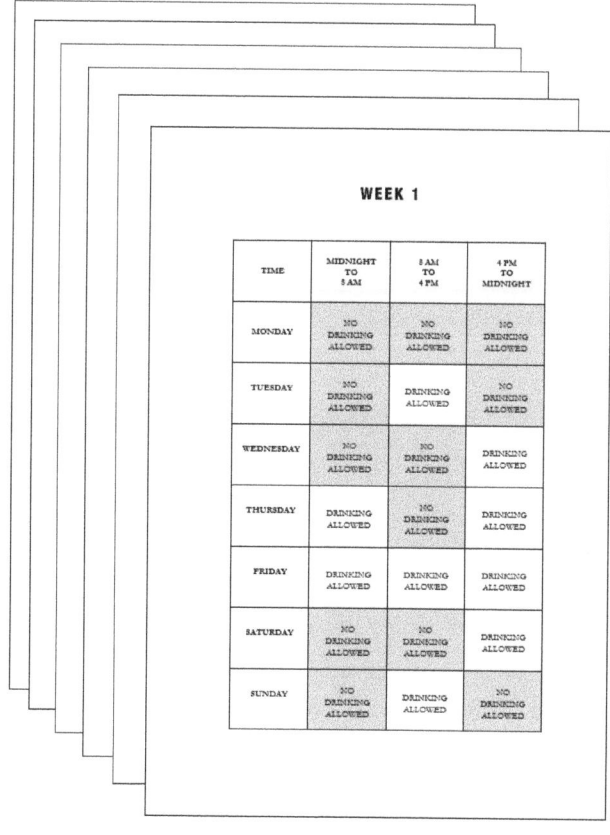

WEEK 1

TIME	MIDNIGHT TO 8 AM	8 AM TO 4 PM	4 PM TO MIDNIGHT
MONDAY	NO DRINKING ALLOWED	NO DRINKING ALLOWED	NO DRINKING ALLOWED
TUESDAY	NO DRINKING ALLOWED	DRINKING ALLOWED	NO DRINKING ALLOWED
WEDNESDAY	NO DRINKING ALLOWED	NO DRINKING ALLOWED	DRINKING ALLOWED
THURSDAY	DRINKING ALLOWED	NO DRINKING ALLOWED	DRINKING ALLOWED
FRIDAY	DRINKING ALLOWED	DRINKING ALLOWED	DRINKING ALLOWED
SATURDAY	NO DRINKING ALLOWED	NO DRINKING ALLOWED	DRINKING ALLOWED
SUNDAY	NO DRINKING ALLOWED	DRINKING ALLOWED	NO DRINKING ALLOWED

But the book is about more than providing a timetable.

We understand ourselves and empower our behaviours when we reason the 'why' behind things.

Accordingly, this book maps out:

1. *Why* you should give the ACR a go
2. *Why* the ACR is so effective at identifying problems with alcohol
3. *Why* alcohol dependency can prove damaging

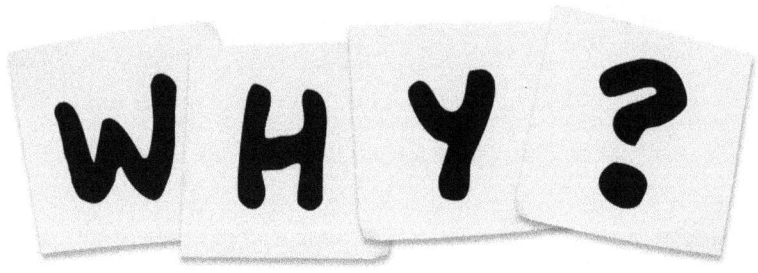

Part 1

What is the ACR?

In a nutshell, it is a simple but highly effective way – over a six-week period of drinking and not drinking – of determining if you have become dependent on alcohol. And, here, dependency means you need alcohol as part of your life; alcohol has a hold over you to some degree.

I think we would all agree that alcohol *is a problem* when you become too dependent upon it; when you come to rely on it to get you through the day, or when it affects different strands in your life. It can impact your health, wealth, happiness, the relationships around you, and much more!

If you are unable to complete the six-week ACR, then your dependency is established. Warning lights should be flashing!

Tell me more about the ACR... and Nick Charles

When I came up with the ACR, I was a homeless, alcoholic vagrant on the streets of London who became obsessed with finding a way that would enable me to drink normally.

"

Alcohol made the very bad times bearable, the bad times good, and the good times even better. Then the wheels came off. The very bad times were unbearable, the bad times dreadful, and the good times unpleasant. And you can't get anywhere without wheels!

"

Nick Charles

On the way to discovering it was impossible to accurately determine those who had crossed the invisible line into addiction, I realised the value of being able to confirm a diagnosis of total dependency.

My initial enthusiasm was shared by an eminent doctor who offered simple healthcare and addiction expertise to itinerant drinkers. He encouraged me to devise a practical plan and the ACR (Alcohol Consumption Regime) was first formed.

The ACR may have had humble beginnings, but it became a much-used tool at the Chaucer Clinic, a rehabilitation and recovery centre I founded in London in 1989. It then established itself as a major feature of the Gainsborough Service, a recovery facility for people with alcohol dependency problems which I set up and ran from 2008 to 2017. Here, I worked in partnership with GPs and patients across Cambridgeshire.

In all, I have been treating dependents for 45 years, and worked in the 'alcohol recovery programme design' arena since 1971 (five years before I stopped drinking). In all of that time, and for the duration of my romance with alcohol, I have never met two alcohol dependents who are the same. In fact, I firmly maintain that they are like fingerprints – each person is unique!

Therefore, it is my aim to fight over time, to change public and professional thinking to refer to those addicted to alcohol as suffering from degrees of alcohol dependency or DAD (as I think of it, with little affection).

The problem with the labels 'Alcoholic' and 'Alcoholism' is that they draw an ugly line in the sand that nobody wants to cross. They help create an 'I ain't got it' indignant denial factor; they imply some sort of character weakness, plus there is the perceived stigma of being seen as an alcoholic.

Alcoholic and Alcoholism are labels as damning as it is possible to be. Although they are widely used, they are inappropriate words – suggesting you either 'are' or you 'are not'. In reality, every person is unique and sits at a different point on the alcohol dependency scale depending on a whole host of factors, including genetics, upbringing, life stresses, access to alcohol, support networks, and more.

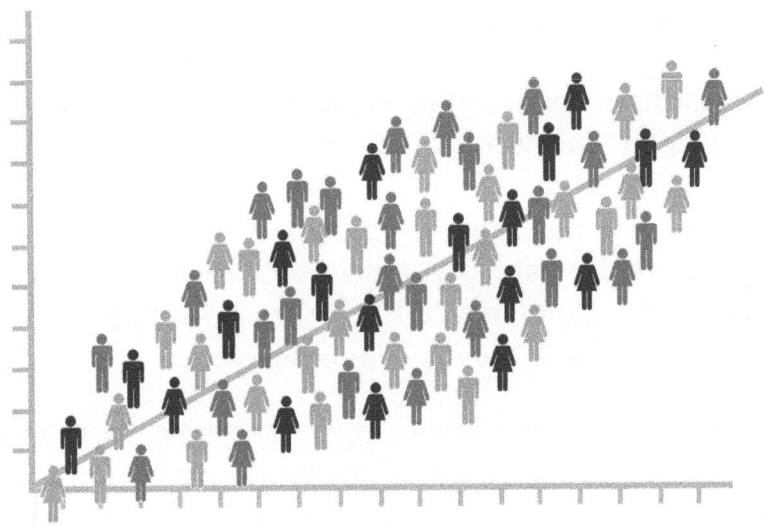

Alcohol dependency is not either/or… it's a scale.

"   **"**

First, you take a drink, then the drink takes a drink, then the drink takes you.

F. Scott Fitzgerald,
The Great Gatsby

The evolution of the ACR

The development of the ACR has been one of stages and change, and to begin with, it was just a three-day affair.

During this short time, if the subject failed to adhere to the clearly marked periods of 'Drinking Allowed' and 'No Drinking Allowed', they were adjudged either powerless over alcohol, or successful in their claims to be in control of their drinking.

As time progressed though, it was revealed that many of the people who found success later admitted they would have failed, had the test lasted for a fourth day. So, the ACR was extended to a week.

A further development came about when the ACR was tested amongst volunteers. It became clear, inadvertently, that the ACR was also a safe and less damaging alcohol consumption regime, an intervention tool in fact. Confident that the ACR now had the capability to both identify dependency and drastically improve health among the alcohol drinking population, it became a three-week review.

But there was more to come. Following research in the late 1990s, the ACR's effectiveness showed a *major improvement* in surveyed outcomes when it became a six-week test. Indeed, recipients were advised to continue using it in a rollover format in order to provide a permanent safeguard.

As touched upon above, what the ACR really highlighted was the idea that there was no such thing as alcoholism, only *degrees* of alcohol dependency.

As time progressed, it transpired that many users of the ACR also encouraged family members who were not heavy drinkers to employ it as a safe method of using alcohol. The reasoning was that it provided a tutorial guide to a safe relationship with alcohol, and many were claiming they presented it to their children, and sooner rather than later.

In recent years A&E hospital departments have used it as part of a friendly warning system; they hand it to those they suspect of incurring injuries while under the influence. Both nursing and doctor staff have applauded the initiative.

What is the logic behind the six-week programme?

We like to see evidence in life – confirmation as to whether our thinking is accurate or inaccurate – and a six-week period of organising and monitoring your drinking patterns will deliver *evidence* of your drinking life. Indeed, to draw upon a legal phrase, the ACR provides this *beyond reasonable doubt*.

Why would the ACR work for me?

Evidence from the ACR that is hard to dispute may not be what you want to hear. Indeed, discovering that you are drinking when you should be abstaining can often be met with firm denial, excuses, even plain disregard.

But there is a simple truth. If you are not able to stick to the ACR, it is plain to see why. And, irrespective of where things go afterwards, a seed will be sown. This food for thought may save your health and years of your life. You can choose to do something on the basis of the evidence you have presented to yourself. Or not, as you see fit.

How can something so simple work?

The ACR's simplicity is its greatest strength. It does not require introspection or soul searching or complex behaviours. It basically just asks you to do one thing – not to drink at certain times of day. By using this focused approach, it is quite clear if a person succeeds or fails.

"   **"**

**For never anything can be amiss,
when simpleness and
duty tender it.**

A Midsummer Night's Dream

What happens when the six weeks end?

That will be up to you. Use the ACR as a forever guide to controlled drinking, perhaps, or come back to the programme after a pre-determined length of time to check that you have not become dependent.

Most importantly, *never* ignore changes in your pattern of drinking. Alcohol addiction is a progressive illness.

What happens if I fail? Do I restart at week one?

Yes. Start again.

It is important that you acknowledge what happened and attempt the ACR once more.

The power of alcohol is firm and fast, yet not everyone has crossed the invisible line into total dependency. The ACR discipline could be your saviour.

If alcohol dependency has not completely taken over in your life, it may have become a serious habit, the strength of which it is possible to weaken. The constant presence of the ACR will instigate a kind of psychological warfare, and the dangers of the one can be overpowered by the common sense of the other (in some cases). The perhaps short periods when you have been able to adhere to the ACR will often yield better quality and less volatile life episodes, and the importance of these moments will register as a plus in your psyche.

Why might I have failed?

The initial obvious, but often incorrect, explanation is that you have crossed a point of no return.

However, this is not necessarily the case, and there is always the possibility that you have developed a destructive habit which is linked to the *feel-good factor.*

Also, powerful and intense friendships exist in the company of fellow drinkers; they are *hail fellow well-met* relationships which are extreme and all-consuming. They are unlike other relationships you will have experienced in the real world, and only found in the favourite living place of the dependent, that is, glass in hand with other full-blown dependents. Should you meet up with any of these people in a sober (alcohol-free) setting, it is unlikely you will have quite so much in common with them, if at all.

What does 'Drinking Allowed' actually mean?

These are designated times, in the ACR, when you are free to drink alcohol, if you so wish. Be mindful that if you drink to excess during these periods, it will almost certainly make it harder to adjust to the 'No Drinking Allowed' slots.

The 'No Drinking Allowed' slots are – as the name suggests – times when alcohol should not be consumed. This is the time when tea, coffee, water, fruit juice, and soft drinks can be enjoyed.

What will help me achieve my controlled drinking goals?

Love, regard, and commitment to loved ones, friends and employers, yet most of all self-respect and (frequently) the promise of peace of mind.

Where can I get more help?

If you have identified that you cannot stick to the ACR, then it is time to seek help. You do not have to rely on yourself; work with others to address your alcohol dependency.

1. Your localities Service Provider via your GP
2. Alcoholics Anonymous.
3. www.alcoholanswers.co.uk
4. There are many useful support groups online

"There's none so blind... as those who will not see!

Drinkers defend alcohol with a fierce determination... while it is systematically destroying them."

Nick Charles

Case Study

Karen was a 42-year-old in an abusive relationship. She drank to hide the pain, and claimed her partner abused alcohol. Indeed, she drank excessively herself to deal with this.

In conversation, Karen asked if there was any way she could prove to her partner that his drinking was the cause of his violence, so the ACR was introduced and she offered it to her partner for them both to take part in a trial run.

The outcome was interesting.

Karen's partner – Michael – became less violent and the relationship improved. He was always very regretful following such incidents, and he agreed to stay with the ACR to save the relationship. They are still together, ten years later, and while they both drink and do not always adhere to the ACR, they do so for the most part. They concede that harmony exists when they do so.

In 2021, both Karen and Michael reported that the ACR is playing a more significant part in their lives as they get older. They stay with it more often than not.

The Mystery of the Door
to the Inner World

I remember, many years ago, when I was finding my way around the mysteries of alcohol addiction, being surprised to discover not everyone got a massive buzz from a drink. In fact, many people only described a feeling of well-being and a little extra confidence after the odd 'one or two'. For me it was like rocket fuel!

It was with this realisation, however, that came the understanding of how one person could become dependent and hopelessly affected, and yet another drink just as regularly yet manage to hold down a regular job. They also seemed to live happily within their domestic environments, although too often appearances proved deceptive. Ultimately, it was revealed that some of these people were just taking a slower road to the same end.

This road is determined by your strength of resistance to dependency, and the best placed person to determine its strength, is you yourself. Only you can judge alcohol's grip on you personally. Be mindful of the door to an inner world where real life does not exist, there really is a point of no return, and the ACR may be trying to tell you something you do not want to hear. Listen to its message, it can bring you the best news you have ever received. For those who feel devastated at the prospect of facing a life alcohol-free, let me assure you all is not lost. You are about to receive an enormous reward.

A fully-recovered alcohol dependent will discover a unique insight into life and human nature, a quality to a degree never found in someone who hasn't had the experience. It's a mixture of wisdom and humility, manifesting itself in a feel for life and its mysteries similar, perhaps, to a God-given gift possessed by a master orator, poet, or philosopher. Once recovered, you've undergone a metamorphosis which has provided an added reverence, and greater profundity.

Part 2

The Alcohol Consumption Regime (ACR) is designed as a diagnosis and intervention tool for those incurring health and social problems by regularly drinking too much.

During its evolution, it has identified those who need to moderate their drinking, as well as those who need to stop consuming alcohol completely. It also offers an awareness indicator to those drinking at increasing and higher risk levels, thus leading to hidden health problems for the future resulting in alcohol-related hospital admissions.

The ideology and versatility of the ACR as an intervention tool, as well as providing a constructive means of diagnosis, offers a discipline for drinkers which will provide them with control over their alcohol consumption, as opposed to them being controlled by it. It has proved to be a vital factor in breaking down the destructive patterns of drinking which leads to dependency, and for exposing potential dependency.

The format is in recurring six-week cycles, which provides a permanent and carefully constructed alcohol consumption schedule. As previously stated, dependent drinking comes about as a result of a destructive pattern of drinking, and for the purposes of identifying any potential or existing alcohol-related health problems, the regime must be followed without deviation for the non-drinking slots.

The drinking slots are not mandatory.

The 24-hour format means that people from all walks of life – working, unemployed, retired, blue or white collar, day and night or shift worker – can use the same regime effectively. In addition to this, it should be noted that where a drinking slot timescale moves into a non-drinking slot (for example, at midnight), this provides a further test of discipline.

The ACR is extremely versatile. With ever-increasing redundancies (not helped, at the time of writing, by the Covid-19 pandemic), people may now face a life without controls, allowing them to stray into a destructive pattern. The ACR provides an early warning indicator for this group, and it also becomes a vital component in preparation for the retired, when there is suddenly more free time – indeed, people are living longer. It also offers a discipline for young people.

The Government/health organisations recommended safe weekly drinking unit levels are ambiguous. Regular drinkers hearing a maximum of 14 units for both men and women immediately see this and other variables as unachievable, so they ignore them completely.

It should be made clear upon introduction to the ACR that it is over and above the 14-unit mark where the alcohol-related health damage begins, and allows drinkers to introduce a discipline based on their own reasoning. It is over these levels that people begin to store up potential alcohol-related chronic or fatal health problems, ultimately resulting in alcohol-related hospital admissions. One of the advantages of the ACR format is that any increase in unit intake makes it more difficult to follow, and the individual's inability to maintain the discipline immediately indicates a potential dependency problem.

The introduction of the ACR will help to reduce the number of people drinking at increasing and higher risk levels.

If the user experiences alcohol withdrawal of any description, they should resume their normal drinking pattern immediately and consult their doctor.

For those unable to adhere to the ACR format, addiction is rearing its ugly head.

The ACR is a simple and easy to use tool that can be given to patients who may want help with their drinking, or to challenge their denial that they have a drink problem.

It is far more realistic than a 14-unit weekly limit, and requires some discipline to reach the end of the six-week challenge. It requires no medication, and will help convince patients and their loved ones that they can control their drinking (or not). It deserves to be widely available.

Dr Arun Aggarwal, Medical Lead
Alcohol Answers Programme

Case Study

It was clear that Megan had a drink problem but – as in lots of cases – she was in serious denial. A fact that was putting her life in danger.

Despite having lost a high-powered career due to her drinking, and had been divorced twice, she refused to acknowledge alcohol was remotely to blame.

Having met in person, we spent a great deal of time counselling to this effect, but Megan refused a detox or any form of treatment.

Megan had been accompanied on the day by her mother, and I briefly explained the ACR to her. I made the point that if proof was needed of her total dependency, her daughter could prove her point by adhering to it.

I was therefore pleased to hear at a later date, that it was Megan's inability to stick to the ACR which convinced her to seek help.

Week 1

TIME	MIDNIGHT TO 8 AM	8 AM TO 4 PM	4 PM TO MIDNIGHT
MONDAY	NO DRINKING ALLOWED	NO DRINKING ALLOWED	NO DRINKING ALLOWED
TUESDAY	NO DRINKING ALLOWED	DRINKING ALLOWED	NO DRINKING ALLOWED
WEDNESDAY	NO DRINKING ALLOWED	NO DRINKING ALLOWED	DRINKING ALLOWED
THURSDAY	DRINKING ALLOWED	NO DRINKING ALLOWED	DRINKING ALLOWED
FRIDAY	DRINKING ALLOWED	DRINKING ALLOWED	DRINKING ALLOWED
SATURDAY	NO DRINKING ALLOWED	NO DRINKING ALLOWED	DRINKING ALLOWED
SUNDAY	NO DRINKING ALLOWED	DRINKING ALLOWED	NO DRINKING ALLOWED

Week 2

TIME	MIDNIGHT TO 8 AM	8 AM TO 4 PM	4 PM TO MIDNIGHT
MONDAY	DRINKING ALLOWED	DRINKING ALLOWED	NO DRINKING ALLOWED
TUESDAY	NO DRINKING ALLOWED	DRINKING ALLOWED	DRINKING ALLOWED
WEDNESDAY	DRINKING ALLOWED	DRINKING ALLOWED	DRINKING ALLOWED
THURSDAY	NO DRINKING ALLOWED	NO DRINKING ALLOWED	NO DRINKING ALLOWED
FRIDAY	DRINKING ALLOWED	NO DRINKING ALLOWED	NO DRINKING ALLOWED
SATURDAY	NO DRINKING ALLOWED	DRINKING ALLOWED	NO DRINKING ALLOWED
SUNDAY	DRINKING ALLOWED	DRINKING ALLOWED	DRINKING ALLOWED

Week 3

TIME	MIDNIGHT TO 8 AM	8 AM TO 4 PM	4 PM TO MIDNIGHT
MONDAY	DRINKING ALLOWED	NO DRINKING ALLOWED	DRINKING ALLOWED
TUESDAY	DRINKING ALLOWED	DRINKING ALLOWED	NO DRINKING ALLOWED
WEDNESDAY	DRINKING ALLOWED	DRINKING ALLOWED	NO DRINKING ALLOWED
THURSDAY	NO DRINKING ALLOWED	DRINKING ALLOWED	DRINKING ALLOWED
FRIDAY	NO DRINKING ALLOWED	NO DRINKING ALLOWED	NO DRINKING ALLOWED
SATURDAY	DRINKING ALLOWED	DRINKING ALLOWED	DRINKING ALLOWED
SUNDAY	NO DRINKING ALLOWED	NO DRINKING ALLOWED	DRINKING ALLOWED

Week 4

TIME	MIDNIGHT TO 8 AM	8 AM TO 4 PM	4 PM TO MIDNIGHT
MONDAY	NO DRINKING ALLOWED	NO DRINKING ALLOWED	NO DRINKING ALLOWED
TUESDAY	NO DRINKING ALLOWED	NO DRINKING ALLOWED	NO DRINKING ALLOWED
WEDNESDAY	NO DRINKING ALLOWED	NO DRINKING ALLOWED	NO DRINKING ALLOWED
THURSDAY	NO DRINKING ALLOWED	NO DRINKING ALLOWED	NO DRINKING ALLOWED
FRIDAY	NO DRINKING ALLOWED	NO DRINKING ALLOWED	NO DRINKING ALLOWED
SATURDAY	DRINKING ALLOWED	DRINKING ALLOWED	DRINKING ALLOWED
SUNDAY	DRINKING ALLOWED	DRINKING ALLOWED	DRINKING ALLOWED

Week 5

TIME	MIDNIGHT TO 8 AM	8 AM TO 4 PM	4 PM TO MIDNIGHT
MONDAY	DRINKING ALLOWED	DRINKING ALLOWED	DRINKING ALLOWED
TUESDAY	DRINKING ALLOWED	DRINKING ALLOWED	DRINKING ALLOWED
WEDNESDAY	DRINKING ALLOWED	DRINKING ALLOWED	DRINKING ALLOWED
THURSDAY	DRINKING ALLOWED	DRINKING ALLOWED	DRINKING ALLOWED
FRIDAY	DRINKING ALLOWED	DRINKING ALLOWED	DRINKING ALLOWED
SATURDAY	NO DRINKING ALLOWED	NO DRINKING ALLOWED	NO DRINKING ALLOWED
SUNDAY	NO DRINKING ALLOWED	NO DRINKING ALLOWED	NO DRINKING ALLOWED

Week 6

TIME	MIDNIGHT TO 8 AM	8 AM TO 4 PM	4 PM TO MIDNIGHT
MONDAY	NO DRINKING ALLOWED	NO DRINKING ALLOWED	NO DRINKING ALLOWED
TUESDAY	NO DRINKING ALLOWED	NO DRINKING ALLOWED	NO DRINKING ALLOWED
WEDNESDAY	NO DRINKING ALLOWED	NO DRINKING ALLOWED	NO DRINKING ALLOWED
THURSDAY	NO DRINKING ALLOWED	NO DRINKING ALLOWED	NO DRINKING ALLOWED
FRIDAY	NO DRINKING ALLOWED	NO DRINKING ALLOWED	NO DRINKING ALLOWED
SATURDAY	NO DRINKING ALLOWED	NO DRINKING ALLOWED	NO DRINKING ALLOWED
SUNDAY	NO DRINKING ALLOWED	NO DRINKING ALLOWED	NO DRINKING ALLOWED

The ACR became a vital tool in my helping people who presented themselves with a drink problem.

Not everybody who drinks needs to stop completely. I found that some people came knowing they had a problem and needed to stop, which usually resulted in a detox. Then, there were the ones who didn't want to stop and I gave them the ACR and saw them weekly for the six weeks. I had success with many, and they were able to change their pattern of drinking. Often, individuals had to do it twice or more times before it helped.

If they failed multiple times, in the main, they decided they would have to stop. Some would say no and went away, and some would return (even over a year later) having discovered there was no way they could control it and decided they needed to cease drinking.

I had a husband and wife come to see me, with the wife saying HE drank too much, and they decided to do the ACR together. As it turned out, it was the WIFE who couldn't do it. This particular couple both stopped. Obviously, if someone came and they were showing signs of alcohol withdrawal, I would NOT recommend the ACR or even mention it.

I always think there should be an alternative to just stopping, and the ACR is perfect to prove whether they have any control remaining or not.

Nikki de Villiers, Alcohol Consultant,
Alcohol Answers Programme

I have worked in Primary Care for 20 years as a frontline manager, and have seen many times the spiral of alcohol addiction lead to great suffering and destruction.

For 12 years, I worked closely with a substance and alcohol misuse GP specialist, and what was painfully evident was the revolving door of treatment that patients experienced. They get ill and are treated in a certain way, and then go out with virtually a sticking plaster over their addiction. Three months later, they return through the revolving door and are back at square one.

I came across the ACR, which was part of a successful recovery programme, and witnessed the beginning of the end of the revolving door syndrome. Here was a tool with the capability of determining the extent of dependency, and it eradicated any chance of a person returning to controlled drinking if they failed the test hopelessly. It also provided a guide to controlled and safe drinking, and a way forward for the futures of young people about to form a relationship with alcohol.

I gave the ACR to a colleague who was an Alcohol Link Worker in the A&E Department at the local hospital, and she thought it wonderful. I got some extra copies, and she said it was the first time her department had something tangible to give to people being discharged following an alcohol-related injury. She was convinced it would have a positive impact on their lives.

Andrew Slater, Business Operations Manager,
WCF West Cambs GP Federation

Part 3

How do I know if a friend or family member has an alcohol problem?

You may be reading this book not for yourself, but because you have concerns about a member of the family, a friend, or another loved one. It may well be alcohol is not just one of the problems in any given life, it could well be that *the* problem in life is alcohol. Here are some of the classic warning signs.

Overwrought behaviour while drinking

Ugly, highly charged emotional behaviour during drinking episodes could be a sign of dependency.

Jekyll and Hyde

The alcohol-fuelled "Jekyll and Hyde" syndrome can result in loud, accusatory lecture-type speech tirades, sudden crying outbreaks, the smashing of furniture, and violence.

The setting for such episodes can vary dramatically from domestic occurrences in the home to serious incidents on aircraft. The extreme behaviour is almost always unprovoked. It is usually triggered by the alcohol's effect on the victim, not by the behaviour of others who happen to be present.

I have met people on several occasions in my life who were so alarmed by the horror of their conduct during and/or after a drinking session, they realised they were seriously affected and opted for an alternative lifestyle and never drank alcohol again.

Non-dependents

Social drinkers (SDs) rarely display nasty behaviour while inebriated. The drunken brawls that occur among young males are an exception. These are more frequent social events (than those of adult SDs) and probably have more to do with crowd psychology and testosterone levels than with alcohol, although the uninhibited effect of booze undoubtedly contributes.

SDs rarely become agitated to the point of rage. When drinking, they are usually more cheerful, and less inhibited than when sober; in the popular apt phrase, they're 'happy.' If they continue drinking, they might fall asleep or get sick – but they don't start breaking chairs.

Alarmingly, the social drinking scene has shifted over the years and particularly during the last two decades.

When I first attended AA meetings in my early troubled years (the middle 1960's and early 1970's), the average age around the table was the 50-60 age group. During the last year of my work in general practice, the average age of my telephone enquiries was 22 years of age in the under 30 age group (the youngest being 14 and the oldest being 30).

The average age of those entering treatment from all enquiries/referrals was 44 years of age. Young people have become more and more likely to succumb than ever before.

Blackouts

These are episodes of amnesia while drinking. It is important to understand the difference between passing out and blacking out.

Passing out is to be unconscious. Blacking out is a state when you appear outwardly normal (if not perhaps a little vague) but have absolutely no knowledge of where you are, what is going on, and later have no recollections of what has taken place during the episode.

Blackouts do not necessarily occur during periods of heavy drinking. More than one dependent (when sober but in-between sessions/binges) has told me a blackout can be triggered by a single drink. However, they are more likely to occur, in my experience, when the victim has been on a prolonged session/binge with little food or nourishment for a prolonged period.

For them to occur during abstinence would be an extremely worrying turn of events, in my view. Blackout episodes can last from a few minutes to several hours or sometimes for much longer periods of time, even for weeks.

During a blackout, the dependent will not necessarily appear drunk and may be capable of functioning at a high level of competency.

Serious mental disturbance

A recovered insurance salesman, looking back on his drinking days, said he had absolutely no recollection of selling the largest policy of his career, and a surgeon who was dependent on alcohol once performed a successful tracheotomy during a blackout. But the scariest blackout story I've heard was of an airline pilot whose blackout ended while he was at the controls of an aeroplane. His most pressing problem was to find out – without alarming his companions in the cockpit – exactly where he was supposed to be flying the plane to!

Benders

These are drinking episodes that last two days or longer, and they continue similarly until the late stages of the disease. Non-dependents do not/cannot drink heavily and continually for two days or longer. Bender/Binge-drinking dependents can and do.

Going on the wagon

People with a dependency on alcohol, sometimes try to prove to themselves (and to others) they are not ruled by alcohol through abstaining. They may stay off booze for weeks, or even months, at a time.

These heavy drinkers, who do not see themselves as full-blown dependents, may cut out alcohol to lose weight, or if they begin to feel unwell. But the necessity they feel for *temporary* cessations may go some way to convince them of a strong indication of total dependency.

The others

Some people inevitably may use more imaginative stratagems.

One female dependent, who was a suburban housewife, voluntarily promised her husband (who had expressed his concern about her heavy drinking) that she would henceforth drink only when entertaining.

Within a matter of weeks, this normally reclusive woman became the most active hostess in the neighbourhood. Dinner party invitations were spewed out to people she barely knew, and to some she couldn't stand. After a few weeks of this frenzied hostessing, she gave up and returned to her normal pattern of drinking… alone.

Sneaky drinking

This is hard to spot, for obvious reasons. One recovered dependent, a salesman, described a technique he used whenever he had lunch with a group of slow-drinking non-dependents. After the first round of drinks was served, he'd gulp his down and then excuse himself to go to the men's room. On the way, he'd stop at the bar and have a quick double. After leaving the men's room, he'd go to the bar again and have a second double. Rejoining his companions with those four extra drinks under his belt, he'd promptly order another round for everyone.

Subterfuge

Closely related to sneaky drinking is the 'secreting' (hiding) of booze. Dependents are fearful of running out of their addictive substance. This leads them to stash bottles away in drawers, on closet shelves and, in particular, if they are living with a concerned non-dependent, in odder places such as inside toilet tanks or in the airing cupboard.

Pre-drinking drinking

When invited to a social event, dependents will prepare themselves against a possible insufficient flow of booze, by drinking before they party. As with other drinking symptoms, this is virtually exclusive to people for whom alcohol has taken a firm grip; non-dependents have no desire, and no need, to pre-drink.

Q: Why do some people become dependent on alcohol, and others seem able to drink without any problems?

*

A: It is a pretty much accepted theory that 'out-of-control dependency' has a strong genetic connection. Alcohol addiction tends to run in families. However, it is important to make the point that all drugs have a dependency factor, and alcohol is most definitely a drug.

Following a lifetime of asking questions of affected people, I believe the genetic influence is irrefutable. To define it, and to make it more understandable, it is where there is a family predisposition to alcohol abuse. As a result of this, a weaker resistance will exist, and therefore a more pronounced 'high' will occur when alcohol is consumed.

Case Study

Dave was 21 and worked in hospitality. He welcomed the ACR, and failed it on three occasions before succeeding.

When he did succeed, he maintained the six-week programme of times when he could and couldn't drink for an extended period, before he slipped.

Soon afterwards, he returned to it and, as a 25-year-old, has confirmed that he still uses the ACR and does not deviate from it, not even for special occasions. Dave claims that alcohol is no longer a problem in his life.

"　　　　　　　　　　　　　　　　**"**

There are as many different alcohol dependents as there are fingerprints on the hands of the human race. We are, therefore, dealing with degrees of alcohol dependence. This will include all those who cannot live without it, no matter how much or little they consume.

Nick Charles

Case Study

Jenny was a 52-year-old divorcee. She was confident of succeeding with the ACR, but failed miserably despite many attempts. Horrified at the thought of never being able to drink alcohol again, she agreed to a complete detox but recommenced drinking immediately afterwards.

Subsequently, Jenny requested a further detox admitting the ACR was crucial at establishing she was totally dependent. There followed three more detoxes, over time, before she achieved total sobriety.

Jenny claims to keep a copy of the ACR regime in a kitchen cupboard. She uses it as a permanent reminder of a low period in her personal history, when she had no control over her alcohol consumption. She has now been alcohol-free for five years.

Dr Marjot's ACR Notes

There are about 40 separate diseases of alcohol, but let's look at three here.

Intoxication

Most drinkers get a tolerance to alcohol, so it seems to take a higher dose to get to previous levels of intoxication. Some drinkers show little or no typical unsteadiness of body, but can still behave in a very disturbed way such as showing aggression or depression.

The picture is partly dependent on the pattern of drinking. At one extreme is the subject who drinks in bouts or benders with intervals of reduced drinking or even abstinence. Such a pattern is described as an ability to abstain, but a loss of control once drinking starts. The other extreme is the continuous drinker who has great difficulty in cutting down or abstaining. The binge drinking pattern tends to shift to continuous drinking over time.

Withdrawal symptoms

Withdrawal symptoms typically include morning nausea, vomiting, and uncontrollable shaking of the hands, and later much of the body. More severe are hallucinations and delusions with agitation, even terror called Delirium Tremens (DTs) as well as epileptic fits. Short-lived mood changes such as anxiety and depression can occur. Such mood changes in both intoxication and withdrawal are almost universally misunderstood as having been seen as the cause NOT THE CONSEQUENCES of heavy drinking. This mistake all too often delays or prevents the proper treatment of the sufferers' diseases of alcohol.

Dependence or addiction

Dependence is used to describe the need to take alcohol to prevent withdrawal symptoms, despite the fact it is known they are harmful quantities. Individuals appreciate the harm they are doing. We often refer to this as a consuming love affair and we have to return to our lover from whom we have parted… come what may! Alcohol addiction is a love affair.

The earliest signs are those of intoxication; not only getting bladdered but losing control. Things can be covered up, and explained away, but problems can arise well before a formal diagnosis will be arrived at.

Degrees of alcohol dependence

Originally, I think we see intoxication as the most conspicuous of behaviours. But the consequences of intoxication can be early, like drink driving, or arrest for drunkenness. Loss of control and a subjective need for alcohol is often early. Withdrawal symptoms are usually later, but morning shakes and sickness can occur early on, as say, after a heavy weekend for instance.

What can I do if I fail the ACR?

Take stock of the reality of your drinking. The ACR shows that loss of control and the compulsive taking of alcohol is coming out on top of your list of priorities and activities.

The choice looks like going on to do more damage or stopping drinking completely. It may be you have tried the ACR on your own, a secret ACR which is like your secret drinking. If you feel as a result you must still try and control your drinking, get the support of other people and be as open about the ACR as possible. A humorous approach involving others may hold the key.

We know that people lose control of their drinking but not always *why*, except that alcohol is one of a number of drugs that can give rise to addiction/dependence. It is clear that alcohol produces a profound change in the brain, for instance fits and DTs in withdrawal. Any sign of such symptoms should be taken seriously and be seen as an indication of a troubled relationship with alcohol. The ACR has done its job, and it is time to seek help.

Dr David Marjot, MB BS. F.R.C. Psych., D.P.M., (retired), Adviser, Alcohol Answers Programme

The Publisher's Story

There was once a publisher who was based in the City of London where he ran his own small publishing company that employed half a dozen people. He was upper-middle aged, set in his ways, and extremely critical of the way the world was changing around him. He didn't own a television set, was resentful of modern music, changing fashion, and what he saw as a lack of respect shown by the younger generation for their elders.

He found his life was made more fraught by the things he hated most. Daily commuting on tube trains which was necessary for him to get to his place of work; they were always overcrowded, hot and stuffy. Most of his staff went to the pub at lunchtime; he had never ever been in a pub and frowned on those who did. He never once considered the fact he took a drink himself, or how often he did so.

As he saw it, life was full of loathsome things, so in order to ease the strain of daily commuting, he got into the habit of secretly drinking a can of lager after breakfast to help him face the tube journey to work. Then, when his secretary came in at 11am with his coffee, he would add brandy when she was out of sight which he extracted surreptitiously from a locked desk drawer to help him through the morning. He would have two brandies of the size you pour yourself when alone at lunch, and then a large shot of brandy in his afternoon tea. Then, there was the evening rush hour to be faced, so he would discreetly down a can of lager. When he reached home, where his wife had prepared his evening meal, she would always give him a large glass of brandy as a nightcap.

Life continued in this regular routine, until one morning when he arrived at the office in great pain. Within an hour of his arrival, he had collapsed onto the floor and was writhing in agony. He was rushed to hospital where it was diagnosed that he had appendicitis, and a routine operation was carried out immediately. The surgery was completed and he came out of the anaesthetic successfully. All seemed to be well. However, within a few hours of recovering from the operation, he began to sweat and shake so badly that a nurse called in a doctor. He could not understand it. Had the patient been in the Far East and caught malaria? He compared notes with an older colleague who recognised the symptoms immediately. He had the publisher placed on appropriate medication and eventually transferred to the detoxification unit of a nearby specialist hospital, where it was confirmed he had been suffering withdrawal symptoms from alcohol.

The publisher was astounded – and his family was too – but a liver scan and subsequent information revealed by the patient confirmed the diagnosis. Eventually, it was necessary for him to undergo a complete change of lifestyle and a form of rehabilitation took place, but the difficulties he encountered abstaining from alcohol convinced him he had become addicted as a result of his drinking over a long period.

The ACR was NOT an option in this case.

"　　　　　　　　　　　　　　　　　　　　**"**

Alcoholism is a baffling illness. It is not like a fracture that can be seen on an X-ray or a tumour that shows up on a scan. It is intangible and the most common symptom is the drinker's denial they are a victim.

Nick Charles

A Drink as Clear as Mud

(The complexities behind dealing with a Way of Life)

In the same way we all go to work but do not necessarily understand each other's occupations, we all enjoy a social life but do not always share each other's choices.

One of my neighbours loves fishing, but I think he is quite mad sitting on a riverbank in the rain under an umbrella for hours on end. Meanwhile, I study alcohol dependency and write books and help drunks, and he thinks I've got a screw loose! The likes and dislikes of other age groups often leave us bewildered. The girl at the stables loves riding horses, and yet her best friend is always on her phone or tablet playing computer games; everyone is different... it's the way of the world.

People who spend hours working out in the gym eating healthily and exercising at every opportunity are horrified by others who spend all their time at home, feet up, watching the telly drinking wine, lager, beer or whatever else. Another group may frequent pubs and restaurants. You will often see them pop outside every half an hour or so to smoke a cigarette and the only exercise they get is going backwards and forwards.

Those keeping fit and living cleanly see the absurdity of a reckless disregard for body and mind. Those who drink regularly are frequently unaware that all alcoholic drinks contain a drug similar to an anaesthetic; so they are not completely conscious of what they do, are never clean of drugs, and so are less capable of good judgement. This is why many of those who recognised alcohol was doing unacceptable things to them stopped using it, and now look back in horror and disbelief at the things they did during their drinking days. Alcohol's effect on people's brains could be likened to the different wavelengths on a radio, where different megahertz send out entirely different programmes. Sinisterly, it takes very little alcohol to switch completely off a one-way-of-thinking station onto another. So should we take a look at our lifestyles, or carry on as we are, or is it already too late? Perhaps it is time to examine the issue more closely.

Let's call those who drink regularly Mr and Mrs Alcohol. If they do so to the point where it becomes troublesome, they may very well recognise their plight and stop drinking. More often than not, they will then view the days when they drank to excess with the same alarm and dismay, as abstainers do who we shall now call Mr and Mrs Clean.

Now, if you think carefully, it is becoming clear that there are two worlds living alongside one another. One which sees through eyes completely unaffected by a drug, and another where a powerful drug called alcohol has completed a mind-altering process. Too often, this is to an extent where it appears perfectly normal to behave in a way that is unacceptable to someone who has not taken alcohol. One is socially acceptable because it does not cause distress or antisocial behaviour, which may affect others. The other sees the world and its rules through a distortion of reality, which refuses to listen to criticism of their behaviour or extreme points of view.

Let us now look even more closely at the place where Mr and Mrs Clean and Mr and Mrs Alcohol live together in a strained atmosphere. It soon becomes clear that there are two additional bewildered parties. One – which we shall call Mr and Mrs What's All the Fuss About – are able to use small amounts of an extremely powerful legal drug called alcohol on rare occasions, and do so enjoyably and acceptably and wonder what on earth all the fuss is about.

Next, there is Mr and Mrs Binger, who never drink from Monday to Thursday, but who – from Friday to Sunday – transform into Jekyll and Hyde, and party recklessly, becoming Mr and Mrs Alcohol for three days only. With no sign of conscience whatsoever, they will unashamedly pretend to be Mr and Mrs What's All the Fuss About from Monday to Thursday, yet they eagerly look forward to Friday when they escape into their inner world.

Worryingly… in prominent positions at the head of this confused community are establishment figures, among whom sit Mr and Mrs Alcohol, Mr and Mrs What's All the Fuss About, Mr and Mrs Binger, and Mr and Mrs Clean. This is why a society which, by and large, likes to drink, see each other through very confused eyes. Depending on which way you view this conundrum, Mr and Mrs Clean can be considered as stuffy stick in the muds, and Mr and Mrs Binger as occasionally mad. Mr and Mrs Alcohol are quite insane and a blot on the landscape, and Mr and Mrs What's All the Fuss About an absolute irritation.

They all sit together confused, and often unhappily, while national confusion and mismanagement reigns supreme; and the reason is quite simple.

Amongst the population, those on drug altered wavelengths are widely represented in government, local councils, law and order, emergency services, health departments and in fact all places of power and responsibility. Indeed, for the most part, the entire populace has as their lover, confidante, and very best friend, the most powerful drug on earth.

*

From this moment onwards alcohol is on trial in your life. The court is in session… and the verdict is yours.

Lightning Source UK Ltd.
Milton Keynes UK
UKHW011135020322
399453UK00001B/50

9 781914 066047